The Consumer-Producer Connection

by Donna Foley

Editorial Offices: Glenview, Illinois • Parsippany, New Jersey • New York, New York
Sales Offices: Needham, Massachusetts • Duluth, Georgia • Glenview, Illinois
Coppell, Texas • Ontario, California • Mesa, Arizona

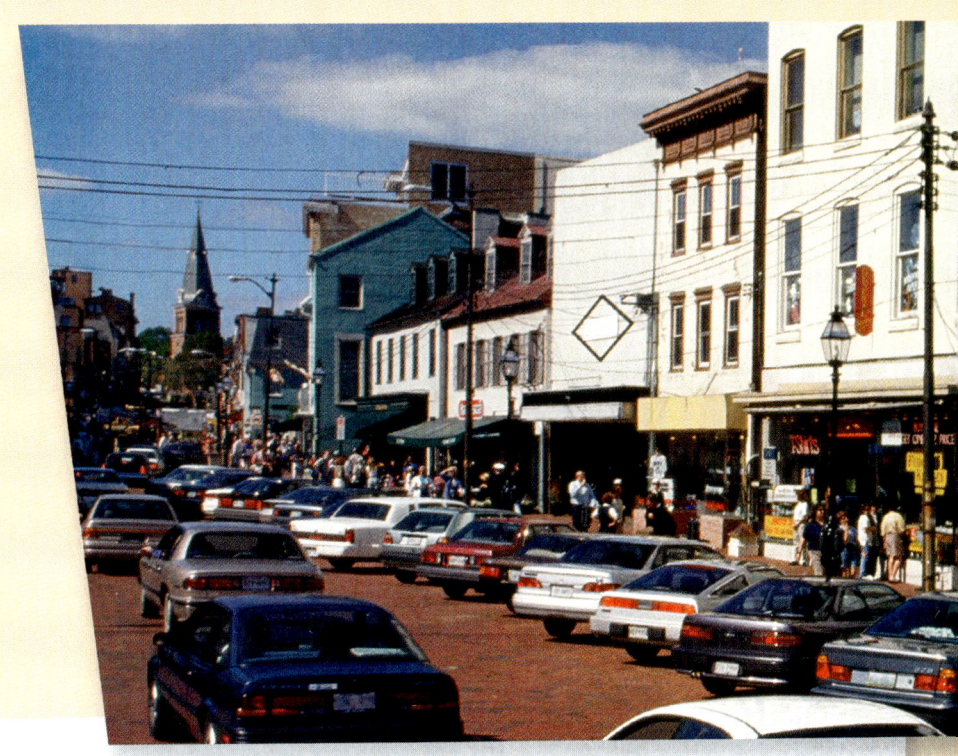

There is a scissor sharpening store in this community. It is connected to other stores in the community. The stores in the community are consumers and producers of **goods** and **services**. Consumers buy services and goods from producers. Producers make goods and services for consumers to buy. Many stores in the community use the services of the scissor sharpening store. Let's see how the consumers and producers in this community work together.

    The store that sells and sharpens scissors is very busy. Customers bring in scissors that need to be sharpened. The store also sharpens gardening tools, knives, and even ice skates. These customers are consumers of the sharpening service.

The scissors that need to be sharpened are brought to the workshop at the store. Small blades are sharpened with hand tools. A sharpening stone may be used to file the edge of the blades. Sometimes a round file is used to sharpen knives. For larger blades, such as gardening tools or ice skates, an electric metal grinder is used.

   Many shop owners use scissors in their businesses. The store sharpens scissors and sells scissors to customers. Different workers need different kinds of scissors. The scissors that a tailor uses are different than the scissors that a florist or a barber uses. The scissor sharpening store has to know how each person uses scissors in their business.

Hair Stylists Use Scissors

One of the shops in this community is a hair styling shop. The stylists use different types of scissors to cut and trim hair. The stylists use the services of the scissor sharpening store because they need sharp scissors to do their job.

Stylists use the sharpened scissors to produce their service, which is haircuts. The scissor sharpening store and the stylists work together to earn an **income**.

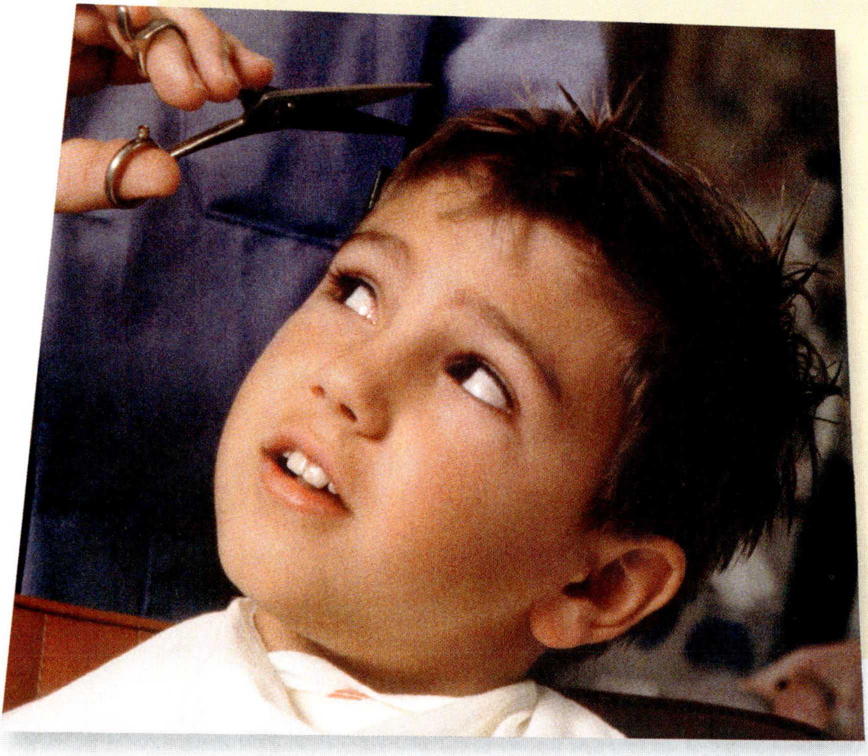

Barbers are also consumers of the scissor sharpening store's services and goods. Barbers need sharp scissors and blades to provide their services. Barbers buy scissors and then use these scissors to sell their haircuts.

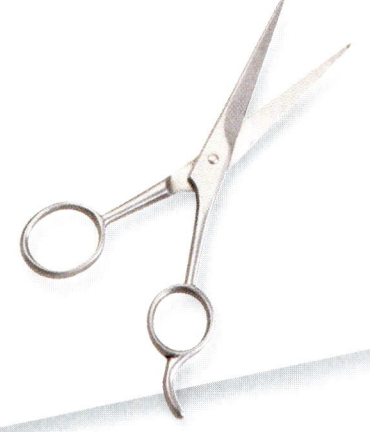

Bakers Use Scissors

The bakery is another shop in the community that buys the scissor sharpening store's services. Bakers need scissors to open packages of ingredients and cut out fancy decorations for their cakes.

The bakery sells its goods to consumers. Customers come into the bakery to buy treats and place special orders. The food that the baker sells is some of the best in town!

The bakery sells some of its goods to coffee shops and restaurants in the community. The coffee shop buys donuts and pastries to sell to its customers. The coffee shop is a consumer of the bakery's goods.

The restaurant buys fresh bread and rolls from the bakery to serve at lunch and dinner. The restaurant is a consumer of the bakery's goods. The restaurant uses goods it has bought to produce tasty meals to sell.

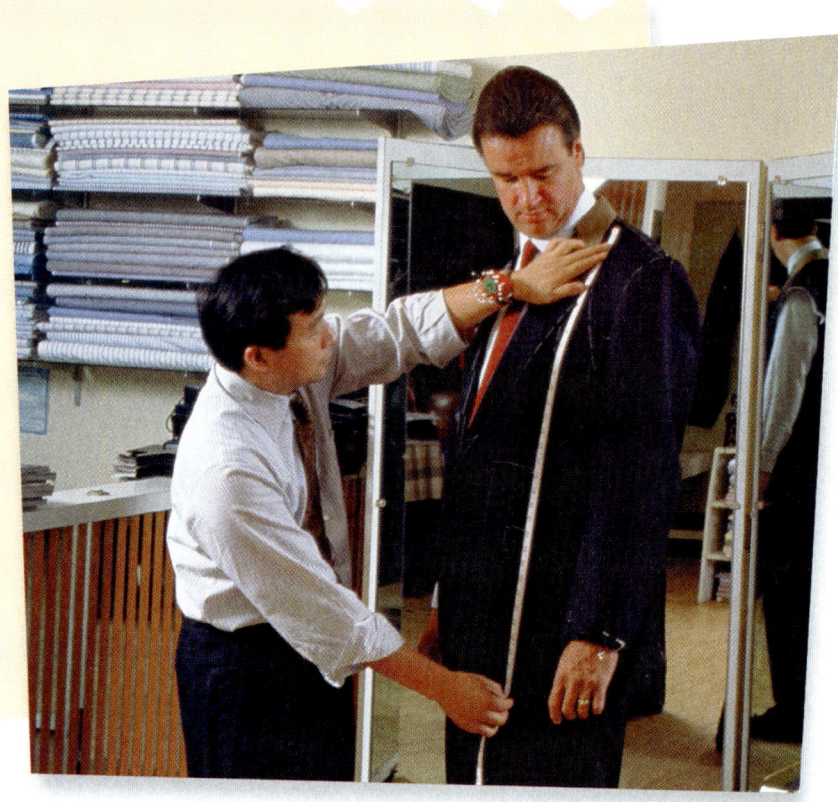

Tailors Use Scissors

Tailors are also consumers of the scissor sharpening shop's services. They need sharp scissors to cut fabric and thread. Tailors provide goods and services to customers and need the services of the scissor sharpening store to do this.

Tailors provide consumers with the service of alterations. When customers buy clothing they sometimes need to have the clothes fixed. Tailors shorten pants and skirts.

Tailors are consumers who buy fabric, thread, buttons, and zippers. Tailors buy these goods to make clothing. Customers order jackets, dresses, and other clothing from the tailor. The tailor makes them so they are just right for the customer.

Tailors are consumers of goods and services for their business. The tailor buys fabric and scissor sharpening services to make goods and services to sell.

Florists Use Scissors

The florist shop is another consumer of the scissor sharpening store's services. Florists need sharp scissors to cut and trim flower stems. They also use scissors to cut ribbons and paper for wrapping flowers and gifts.

Florists are also consumers of fresh flowers. Florists buy the flowers from a flower seller. Florists then use the flowers to make goods for customers.

Customers buy flowers to decorate their homes, to celebrate special days, or to cheer up sick friends. Florists need the scissor sharpening store's service to do their jobs.

Florists are consumers when they buy flowers, ribbon, and other supplies. Florists are producers when they sell their goods to customers. Everyone loves to visit the sweet-smelling florist shop!

A Community Celebration

Tonight, there is a party for all the store owners in the community. They are celebrating their hard work. Everyone brings something to make it a special evening. The florist brings flowers. The baker brings cakes and trays of cookies.

The shop owners and customers in the community are all connected. The shops are consumers of goods and services. They use these goods and services in their businesses. The shops then sell their goods and services to customers in the community.

Almost everyone in the community is both a consumer and a producer. The customers are consumers of goods sold in the shops. The shops are consumers of the goods and services they need. Everyone works together to buy and sell what they need.

Glossary

goods things that people make or grow

income money that someone earns

service job that people do to help others

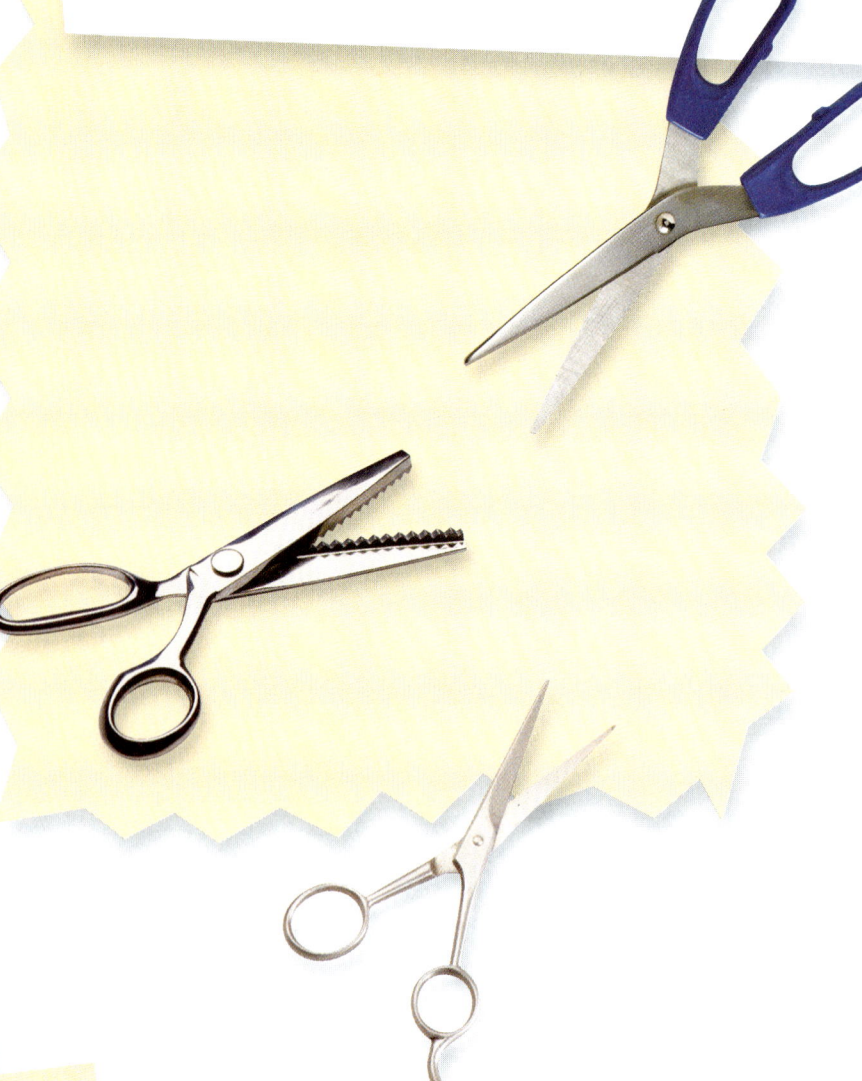